Just like you

written by Kaitlyn Mamay
Illustrated by Patricia Olstad

Just Like You
Text copyright © 2017 Kaitlyn Mamay
Illustrations copyright © 2024 Patricia Olstad
Art photography by Gary Mamay gary@mamayphoto.com

Bounceberry Books

New York, NY · First edition · Published September 2024

Dedicated to

every child with cancer who has ever
felt different... and their friends!

Just like you...

I just want to be a kid.

Just like you...

I like hugs, cancer is not contagious!

Just like you...

I get scared.

Just like you...

sometimes I don't feel like talking.

Just like you...

I like to laugh and play with my friends.

and...

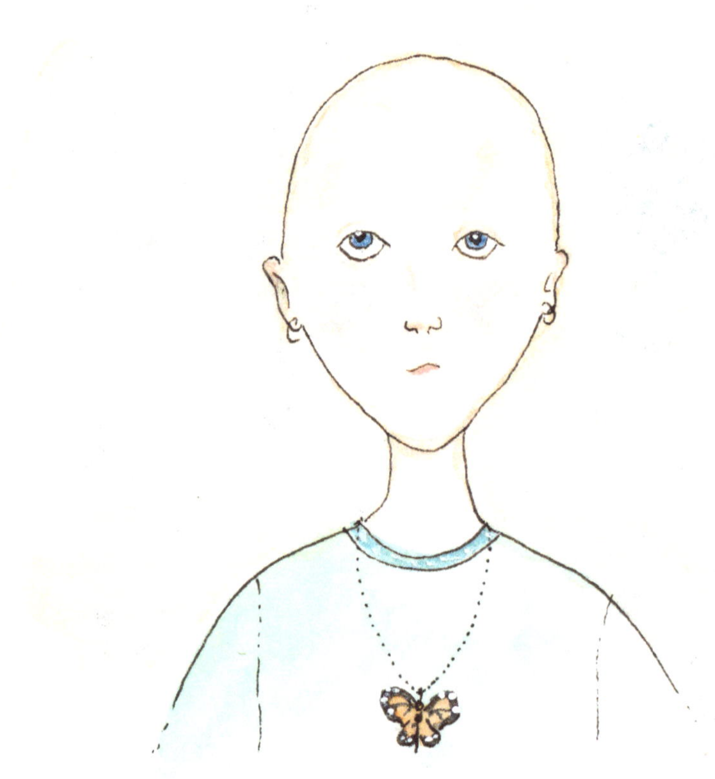

I may be missing all my hair...

but I'm just like you.

I may spend my holidays beside
doctors and nurses...

but I'm just like you.

I may know the names of more chemotherapies than state capitals...

but I'm just like you.

I may have to use a wheelchair
to get around...

but I'm just like you.

I may spend more time at the
hospital than at school...

but I'm just like you.

So when you see me, just remember...

I'm just like you!